CHINESE

C·O·O·K·I·N·G
Exciting Ideas for Delicious Meals

Photography by Peter Barry and Jean-Paul Paireault
Recipes by Lalita Ahmed, Carolyn Garner, Moyra Fraser
    and Frederic Lebain
Designed by Richard Hawke
Edited by Jillian Stewart
3256
This edition published 1996 by Bramley Books
© Bramley Books, Godalming, Surrey
Printed and bound in Hong Kong
ISBN 1-85833-530-2

CHINESE
C·O·O·K·I·N·G
Exciting Ideas for Delicious Meals

Bramley Books

Contents

Introduction

Most of us will never travel to China, but we can enjoy the country's delicious and varied dishes without leaving our own kitchens. China is a vast country and its sheer size is one of the key elements in the success of this wonderful cuisine. Because of its great land area, China has a diverse range of climates and crops, hence a plethora of regional specialities.

In the South, the weather is warm and the meals light. Stir-fried dishes with crisp vegetables are popular and rice is the staple. It is this style that we are most familiar with in the West as most of the Chinese communities which have settled overseas are from this area. Canton in particular is at the heart of this tradition and many dishes such as stir-fried rice and sweet and sour dishes originated here. By contrast, the North is a cold, wheat growing region which has a hearty, warming cuisine. Noodles are eaten more often than rice, rich sauces and meat dishes are popular as are pancakes and dumplings. It is from this area that the legendary Peking Duck originates.

In the East, the mild climate and fertile soil mean that both rice and wheat grow well and rice and noodles compete equally for popularity. Seafood and freshwater fish are very popular and it is here that some of China's most popular fish: carp, shad, bream and perch, are found in abundance. Noodles combined with seafood or poultry are particular favourites in tea houses. In the western provinces it is strong spicy flavours which predominate rather than the fresh, light flavours of the East. Szechuan cuisine, as it is known, has become increasingly popular in this country, its spicy, hearty flavours endearing it to a growing number of devotees.

The techniques used in Chinese cooking are crucial to the final taste and look of a dish. Stir-frying is probably the most important Chinese cooking method and to this end a wok is best, but a large heavy-based saucepan can be used. Some of the ingredients may not be familiar, but if you do not have a Chinese supermarket within easy reach there are easy alternatives which are readily available. Cooking Chinese food takes only minutes for most recipes, but preparation often involves much slicing and chopping, so it is best to have everything ready before you begin cooking. Ingredients are generally cut to approximately the same size so that they cook in the same amount of time.

Chinese cooking remains one of the most popular ways of eating out simply because it is simple, tasty and varied. So try bringing a taste of China into your cooking, and with a bit of practice China will not be so far away.

NOODLES IN SOUP

A simple soup which is nonetheless tasty.

SERVES 4-6

450g/1lb small rounds of noodle cakes
Salt
1.3ltrs/2¼ pints chicken or beef broth, or
   thick stock
100g/4oz cooked shredded chicken
100g/4oz Chinese napa cabbage, finely
   shredded (or iceberg lettuce)
2 spring onions, thinly sliced
2 eggs, hard boiled and sliced

1. Cook the noodles in boiling, salted water for 5 minutes. Drain thoroughly.

2. Heat the broth or stock and add salt to taste. Add the cooked noodles, chicken, cabbage and spring onions, and heat gently for 1 minute.

3. Transfer the soup to serving bowls and garnish with the sliced eggs if desired.

TIME: Preparation takes 10 minutes, cooking takes 6-8 minutes.

BUYING GUIDE: Noodles are available in different thicknesses – buy the thinest for soups.

PEKING-STYLE SOUP

Duck stock is the basis of this tasty, filling soup, which contains meat and vegetables, and is delicately flavoured with sesame seeds and soy sauce.

SERVES 4

4 slices smoked ham
1 head Chinese cabbage
850ml/1½ pints duck stock
1 tbsp sesame seeds
Pinch chopped garlic
15ml/1 tbsp soy sauce
½ tsp white wine vinegar
Salt and pepper
1 egg yolk, beaten

1. Cut the ham into small, even-sized cubes.

2. Cut the Chinese cabbage into small pieces and simmer briskly for 10 minutes in the duck stock.

3. Stir in the sesame seeds, garlic, ham, soy sauce, vinegar and salt and pepper to taste.

4. Cook for 10 minute over a gentle heat. Using a teaspoon, drizzle the beaten egg yolk into the soup. Serve immediately.

TIME: Preparation takes about 5 minutes and cooking takes approximately 20 minutes.

VARIATION: Replace the smoked ham with a different smoked meat.

WATCHPOINT: The smoked ham is likely to change colour during cooking.

CRAB AND WATERCRESS SOUP

Crab and watercress make a great combination in this quick soup.

SERVES 4-6

1½ ltrs/2½ pints chicken stock
100g/4oz white crab meat, shredded
2 spring onions, finely chopped
2 bunches watercress, finely chopped
Salt and freshly ground black pepper to
    taste
5g/1 tsp cornflour or arrowroot
15ml/1 tbsp water
10ml/2 tsps light soy sauce
A few drops sesame oil

1. Bring the stock to the boil with the crab meat, onions and watercress and simmer for 4-5 minutes. Add salt and pepper to taste.

2. Mix the cornflour with the water and add to the soup. Allow to simmer for a further 2 minutes.

3. Add soy sauce and sesame oil, mix well and simmer for 2 minutes. Serve immediately.

TIME: Preparation takes 10 minutes, cooking takes 8-9 minutes.

BUYING GUIDE: Ensure the watercress is not limp – it deteriorates rapidly once it reaches the supermarket.

CURRY SOUP WITH MEATBALLS

A hearty soup which is perfect for heating up a cold winter night.

SERVES 4

Meatballs
225g/8oz lean minced beef
1 clove garlic, crushed
1 onion, peeled and finely chopped
½ tsp salt
½ tsp curry powder, or ¼ tsp curry paste
½ tsp ground cinnamon
½ tsp ground cloves
½ tsp ground pepper
30g/1oz breadcrumbs
1 small egg, lightly beaten

Peanut oil

Broth
5g/1 tsp garam masala
5g/1 tsp turmeric
1 onion, peeled and finely chopped
1 tsp curry leaves
570ml/1 pint water
1 clove garlic, crushed
½ cup desiccated coconut, soaked in 1
  cup hot water for 15 minutes.

1. Mix together meatball ingredients, and form into small balls about the size of walnuts.

2. Heat wok, add oil and, when hot, fry meatballs. When browned well all over, remove with a slotted spoon, and drain on absorbent paper.

3. Carefully drain oil from wok. Add 5ml/1 tsp of oil, and fry spices for the broth for 30 seconds.

4. Add onion, curry leaves, and garlic, and cook together for 3 minutes.

5. Meanwhile, strain coconut in a sieve, press out as much liquid as possible, and discard the pulp.

6. Add water and coconut milk to the wok and simmer together for 5 minutes.

7. Adjust seasoning. Strain soup and return to wok. Add meatballs and simmer a further 5 minutes. Serve hot.

TIME: Preparation takes 30 minutes, cooking takes 20 minutes.

BUYING GUIDE: You will often find curry leaves in jars on the spice counter in supermarkets.

BAMBOO SHOOT SOUP

*A very decorative soup. Beaten egg sifted into the hot
soup gives a very special effect.*

SERVES 4

90g/3oz bamboo shoots, cut into thin
    matchsticks
4 dried Chinese black mushrooms, soaked
    for 15 minutes in warm water
850ml/1½ pints chicken stock
15ml/1 tbsp wine vinegar
30ml/2 tbsps light soy sauce
Salt and pepper
½ tsp cornflour, combined with a little
    water
1 egg
10 chives

1. Blanch the bamboo shoots in boiling,
salted water for 3 minutes. Rinse and set
aside to drain.

2. Cook the mushrooms in boiling, salted
water for 10 minutes. Rinse and set aside
to drain.

3. Bring the stock to the boil and add the
bamboo shoots, mushrooms, vinegar, and
soy sauce and season with salt and
pepper to taste. Cook for 10 minutes.

4. Stir in the cornflour and bring the soup
slowly back to the boil.

5. Reduce the heat. Beat the egg
thoroughly. Place the beaten egg in a
sieve and add to the soup by shaking the
sieve back and forth over the hot soup.

6. Add the chives to the soup and serve
piping hot.

TIME: Preparation takes about 5 minutes and cooking takes approximately 30 minutes.

WATCHPOINT: Make sure the soup is boiling hot before adding the beaten egg.

COOK'S TIP: Try to buy fresh chives for this soup, as they have a
much better flavour than dried chives.

TURKEY SOUP WITH BLACK MUSHROOMS

An unusual blend of flavours which makes a tasty, warming soup.

SERVES 4

175g/6oz turkey breast meat
15ml/1 tbsp sesame oil
50g/2oz dried Chinese black mushrooms,
   soaked for 15 minutes in warm water
850ml/1½ pints chicken stock
15ml/1 tbsp soy sauce
1 slice fresh root ginger
Salt and pepper

1. Cut the turkey meat into slices and then into small cubes.

2. Heat the sesame oil in a wok and stir-fry the meat until brown. Remove from the pan and drain off any excess oil.

3. Cook the mushrooms in boiling, salted water for 10 minutes. Rinse and drain well.

4. Place the mushrooms in a saucepan with the stock. Stir in the meat, soy sauce, ginger and salt and pepper to taste.

5. Bring to the boil and then simmer gently for 15 minutes.

6. Remove the slices of ginger just before serving. Serve the soup piping hot.

TIME: Preparation takes about 8 minutes and cooking takes approximately 35 minutes.

SERVING IDEA: Sprinkle the soup with 1 tbsp chopped fresh chives before serving.

WATCHPOINT: Don't forget to remove the slice of ginger before serving.

SWEETCORN AND CHICKEN SOUP

A classic soup which is still a great favourite.

SERVES 4

1 chicken, with giblets
225g/8oz can creamy sweetcorn
1 onion, peeled and chopped roughly
1 carrot, scraped and chopped roughly
1 stick celery, chopped
6 peppercorns
Parsley stalks
1 bay leaf
1 ltr/2 pints water
Salt
Pepper

Garnish
Chopped parsley or chives

1. Clean chicken, and cut into quarters. Put into wok with giblets, chopped vegetables, peppercorns, bay leaf, parsley stalks, seasoning and water.

2. Bring to the boil. Reduce heat and simmer for 30 minutes. Strain and return stock to wok.

3. Discard the vegetables and giblets. Remove meat from chicken and cut into fine shreds.

4. Add undrained sweetcorn to stock, and bring to boil. Simmer for 5 minutes.

5. Add chicken and cook for 1 minute.

6. Sprinkle with chopped parsley or chives. Serve hot.

TIME: Preparation takes 15 minutes, cooking takes 45 minutes.

CRAB SOUP WITH GINGER

*This delicately flavoured soup, with fresh crab and a
hint of ginger, is perfect for serving at a special dinner.*

SERVES 4

1 carrot, chopped
1 onion, chopped
½ leek, chopped
1 bay leaf
2 medium-sized crabs
850ml/1½ pints fish stock
1-inch piece of fresh ginger root, chopped
5ml/1 tsp Sake Chinese wine (optional)
Salt and pepper

1. Make a vegetable stock by putting the
carrot, onion, leek and bay leaf into a
saucepan with a large quantity of water.
Bring to the boil and add the crabs. Allow
to boil briskly for 20 minutes or until
cooked.

2. Remove the crabs when cooked and
allow to cool. Once cooled, break off the
pincers and break the joints, cut open the
back and open the claws. Carefully
remove all the crab meat.

3. Bring the fish stock to the boil and add
the ginger, Sake and the crab meat. Boil
for 15 minutes.

4. Check the seasoning, adding salt and
pepper as necessary. Serve very hot.

TIME: Preparation takes about 40 minutes and cooking takes approximately 35 minutes. It
takes about 30 minutes for the crab to cool, before you can comfortably
remove the meat with your fingers.

WATCHPOINT: Allow plenty of time for opening the crab and removing all the meat. If
time does not permit preparing fresh crab, use canned crab meat.

COOK'S TIP: Prepare the soup the day before serving. If allowed to rest overnight, the
flavour of the soup will develop deliciously. Reheat gently just before serving.

SHRIMP FU YUNG

This dish is perfect for lunch or an evening snack.

SERVES 4-6

Oil
1-2 cloves of garlic, chopped
100g/4oz prawns, peeled
100g/4oz green beans, sliced
1 carrot, shredded
6 eggs
Salt and freshly ground black pepper to
   taste
225ml/8 fl oz chicken stock
¼ tsp salt
10ml/2 tsps soy sauce
5ml/1 tsp sugar
5ml/1 tsp cornflour

1. Heat 30ml/2 tbsps oil in a wok. Add the garlic and stir-fry for 1 minute.

2. Add the prawns and stir-fry for 1 minute.

3. Add the beans and carrots and stir-fry for 2 minutes. Remove and keep on one side.

4. Beat the eggs with salt and pepper to taste, and add the cooled shrimp mixture.

5. Clean the wok and heat 5ml/1 tsp oil. Pour 60ml/4 tbsps of the egg mixture and cook like a pancake. When the egg is set, turn the pancake over and cook on the other side until lightly golden. Place on a warm platter and keep warm.

6. To make the sauce beat the stock with the other sauce ingredients and stir over a gentle heat until the sauce thickens. Serve the pancakes with this sauce.

TIME: Preparation takes 10 minutes, cooking takes 4 minutes for filling/
3-4 minutes for each pancake.

THE PEKING DUCK

A magnificent recipe much loved by all fans of Chinese cooking.

SERVES 6

1 duck, weighing 4lbs
½ medium cucumber
4 spring onions

Sauce
Small can yellow bean sauce
45g/3 tbsps sugar
30ml/2 tbsps oil

1. Clean and dry the duck. Leave in a cool place overnight.

2. Finely shred the cucumber and spring onions.

3. Preheat the oven to 200°C/400°C/Gas mark 6. Place the duck on a grill rack set on top of a baking pan. Cook the duck for 1¼ hours. The duck should be very dark and crispy.

4. For the sauce, heat 2 tbsps oil in a small pan. Add the yellow bean paste and sugar. Cook together for 1-2 minutes.

5. Peel the skin off the duck and cut into 2-inch slices. Serve on a heated platter. Carve the meat off the duck into 2-inch slices, serve on a separate platter.

6. The duck skin and meat are eaten by wrapping them in pancakes which are first of all brushed with a teaspoon of duck sauce and a layer of cucumber and spring onions.

TIME: Preparation takes about 15 minutes, cooking takes nearly 2 hours.

BUYING GUIDE: More and more supermarkets are stocking a wide range of Chinese sauces, such as yellow bean.

RICE PAPER PRAWN PARCELS

The perfect nibble for a drinks party.

MAKES ABOUT 20 PARCELS

225g/8oz prawns, shelled and de-veined
1 egg white
½ tsp cornflour
5ml/1 tsp Chinese wine, or 10ml/2 tsps
   dry sherry
5g/1 tsp sugar
5ml/1 tsp light soy sauce
6 spring onions, finely sliced
Salt
Pepper
140ml/¼ pint peanut oil
1 packet rice paper

1. Dry prepared prawns on absorbent paper.

2. Mix egg white, cornflour, wine, sugar, soy sauce, spring onions and seasoning together. Mix in prawns.

3. Heat peanut oil in wok until hot.

4. Wrap five or six prawns in each piece of rice paper.

5. Gently drop in rice paper parcels and deep fry for about 5 minutes. Serve hot.

TIME: Preparation takes 15 minutes, cooking takes 15 minutes.

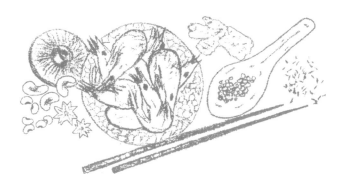

SCRAMBLED EGGS WITH PRAWNS

Fish-flavoured scrambled eggs, cooked with prawns.

SERVES 4

12 prawns, peeled
8 eggs, beaten
½ stick celery, cut into small dice
1 spring onion, chopped
5ml/1 tsp fish sauce
Salt and pepper

1. Cut the prawns into small pieces.

2. Stir the prawns into the eggs and add the celery, spring onion and fish sauce.

3. Season with a little salt and pepper.

4. Cook by stirring over a gentle heat. When cooked to your liking, serve immediately.

TIME: Preparation takes about 10 minutes and cooking takes approximately 10 minutes.

SZECHUAN BANG BANG CHICKEN

This is a good dish to serve as a starter.

SERVES 2

2 chicken breasts
1 medium cucumber

Sauce
60g/4 tbsps peanut butter
10ml/2 tsps sesame oil
½ tsp sugar
¼ tsp salt
10ml/2 tsps stock
½ tsp chilli sauce

1. Simmer the chicken in a pan of water for 30 minutes. Remove the chicken breasts and cut them into ½-inch thick strips.

2. Thinly slice the cucumber. Spread cucumber on a large serving platter. Pile the shredded chicken on top.

3. Mix the peanut butter with the sesame oil, sugar, salt and stock. Pour the sauce evenly over the chicken.

4. Sprinkle the chilli sauce evenly over the top.

TIME: Cooking takes about 30 minutes, final preparation takes 5 minutes.

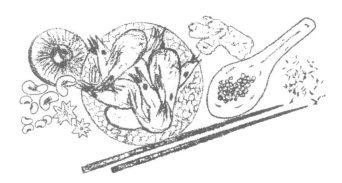

Sesame Prawn Toasts with Crispy Seaweed

Have great fun trying to eat crispy seaweed with your chopsticks!

SERVES 2-4

100g/4oz pork fat
175g/6oz cooked prawns
1 egg white
Salt and pepper to taste
15g/1 tbsp cornflour
2 slices white bread
90g/6 tbsps sesame seeds
Oil for deep frying

Crispy Seaweed
2lbs greens
60g/4 tbsps split almonds
Oil for deep frying
½ tsp salt
7.5g/1½ tsps sugar

1. Finely chop pork fat and prawns. Blend together well with egg white, salt, pepper and cornflour. Spread the 'paste' thickly on the 2 slices of bread. Remove the crusts.

2. Sprinkle the paste thickly with sesame seeds pressing them on well.

3. Heat the oil. Lower one slice of bread at a time into the hot oil, spread side down, for 2 minutes. Turn over and fry the other side for ½ minute. Repeat for other slice of bread.

4. Cut each prawn toast in half, then into finger sized strips.

5. With a very sharp knife, cut the greens into the finest shreds possible. Dry, by spreading them out on kitchen paper for ½ hour. Deep fry, or shallow fry the almonds until golden. Drain well.

6. Heat the oil until it is about to smoke. Remove from the heat for ½ minute.

7. Add all the shreds of greens. Stir and return pan to the heat and fry for 2-3 minutes. Remove and drain well.

8. Serve the prawn toasts and crispy seaweed on a well heated platter, sprinkle crispy seaweed evenly with salt, sugar, and almonds.

TIME: Preparation takes 10 minutes for the prawn toasts and 5 minutes for the seaweed, cooking takes about 10 minutes for the prawn toasts and about 3 minutes for the crispy seaweed.

BUYING GUIDE: Sesame seeds can be bought from health food stores as well as some good supermarkets.

SEAFOOD CHOW MEIN

Chinese noodles cooked with mussels, cockles and vegetables and served in a rich ginger and wine flavoured sauce.

SERVES 4

225g/8oz Chinese noodles
½ green pepper, seeded
½ red pepper, seeded
15ml/1 tbsp oil
½ tsp chopped garlic
½ tsp chopped fresh ginger root
½ spring onion, chopped
125g/5oz uncooked mussels (shelled)
50g/2oz uncooked cockles (shelled)
15ml/1 tbsp Chinese wine
30ml/2 tbsps soy sauce
Salt and pepper

1. Cook the noodles in boiling, salted water. Rinse them under cold water and set aside to drain.

2. Cut the peppers into thin slices.

3. Heat the oil in a wok and stir-fry the garlic, ginger, peppers and spring onion for 1 minute.

4. Stir in the mussels, cockles, Chinese wine, soy sauce and the cooked noodles.

5. Mix together well, using chopsticks. Season with salt and pepper and serve when cooked through completely.

TIME: Preparation takes about 15 minutes and cooking takes approximately 15 minutes.

VARIATION: Add other types of seafood to this dish.

WATCHPOINT: In Step 5 heat the noodles thoroughly, turning them in the sauce, to coat evenly.

SZECHUAN FISH STEAK

Szechuan food is hot and this recipe makes a wonderfully zippy fish dish.

SERVES 4

675g/1½lbs haddock
10g/2 tsps salt
30g/2 tbsps cornflour
1 egg

Sauce
1 large onion
2 cloves garlic
3 slices ginger root
2 chilli peppers
2 slices Szechuan Ja Chai pickle (see
    Cook's Tip)
1 dried chilli
Oil for deep frying
90ml/6 tbsps chicken stock
45ml/3 tbsps soy sauce
30g/2 tbsps tomato paste
30ml/2 tbsps Hoisin sauce
15g/1 tbsp sugar
15ml/1 tbsp wine vinegar
30ml/2 tbsps pale sherry

1. Cut fish into 2 x 1-inch oblong pieces. Rub with salt. Blend the cornflour with the egg. Dip the fish in the egg mixture to coat on both sides.

2. Thinly slice the onion. Finely chop the garlic, ginger, chillies, pickle and dried chilli.

3. Heat 4 tbsps oil in a large frying pan. Add the onion and other chopped vegetables; stir-fry for 2 minutes.

4. Add the stock, soy sauce, paste, Hoisin sauce, sugar, vinegar, and sherry. Stir them over a high heat until well reduced.

5. Heat about 4 cups oil in a deep fryer. When hot, add the fish and fry for 2 minutes. Remove and drain.

6. Place them in the pan of sauce. Simmer in the sauce for 5 minutes before serving.

TIME: Preparation takes 10 minutes, cooking takes 10 minutes.

COOK'S TIP: If you cannot obtain the Ja Chai pickle, substitute your favourite hot pickle.

STEAMED PRAWNS

*Fresh prawns, garnished with courgette peel, steamed
and served with a fish-flavoured sauce.*

SERVES 4

15ml/1 tbsp fish sauce
5ml/1 tbsp water
15ml/1 tbsp wine vinegar
15ml/1 tbsp soy sauce
10g/2 tsps sugar
10 fresh mint leaves, finely chopped
1 shallot, chopped
Salt and pepper
12 fresh prawns, peeled and cleaned
2 medium-sized courgettes, peeled and
    the peel cut into long strips

1. Mix together the fish sauce, water,
vinegar, soy sauce, sugar, mint, shallot
and salt and pepper. Stir well and set
aside for a least 1 hour.

2. Just before serving time, season the
prawns with plenty of salt and pepper.

3. Roll the strips of courgette peel around
the prawns and cook them in a Chinese
steamer for 5 minutes.

4. Serve the prawns piping hot,
accompanied with the sauce.

TIME: Preparation takes about 20 minutes and cooking takes about
10 minutes for 2 batches.

COOK'S TIP: If the strips of courgette peel are not very pliable, blanch them in boiling
water for 3 seconds, before wrapping around the prawn.

WATCHPOINT: The sauce can be prepared just before cooking the prawn, but it is much
tastier if prepared at least 1 hour in advance.

Honey Sesame Prawns

Prawns sweetened with honey and sprinkled
with sesame seeds – the perfect dish to spoil yourself with.

SERVES 4

100g/4oz self-raising flour
Pinch of salt
Pepper
1 egg, lightly beaten
140ml/¼ pint water
450g/1lb prawns shelled and de-veined
30g/2 tbsps cornflour
Oil for deep frying
15ml/1 tbsp sesame oil
30g/2 tbsps honey
15g/1 tbsp sesame seeds

1. Sift flour and salt and pepper into a bowl. Make a well in the centre, add egg and water, and gradually mix in the flour.

2. Beat to a smooth batter and set aside for 10 minutes.

3. Meanwhile, toss prawns in cornflour and coat well. Shake off any excess cornflour. Add prawns to batter and coat well.

4. Heat oil in wok and add prawns, a few at a time. Cook until batter is golden. Remove prawns, drain on absorbent paper, and keep warm. Repeat until all prawns have been fried.

5. Carefully remove hot oil from wok. Gently heat sesame oil in pan.

6. Add honey and stir until mixed well and heat through. Add prawns to mixture and toss well.

7. Sprinkle over sesame seeds and again toss well. Serve immediately.

TIME: Preparation takes 20 minutes, cooking takes 20 minutes.

CRISPY FISH WITH CHILLI

Choose your favourite white fish for this recipe.

SERVES 4

450g/1lb fish fillet, skinned, bones removed, and cut into 2.5cm/1-inch cubes

Batter
60g/2oz plain flour
1 egg, separated
15ml/1 tbsp oil
75ml/5 tbsps milk
Salt
Oil for deep frying

Sauce
5g/1 tsp grated root ginger
¼ tsp chilli powder
30g/2 tbsps tomato purée
30g/2 tbsps tomato chutney
30ml/2 tbsps dark soy sauce
30ml/2 tbsps Chinese wine or dry sherry
30ml/2 tbsps water
5g/1 tsp sugar

1 red chilli, seeds removed, and sliced finely
1 clove garlic, crushed
Salt
Pepper

1. Sift the flour with a pinch of salt. Make a well in the centre, and drop in the egg yolk and oil.

2. Mix to a smooth batter with the milk, gradually incorporating the flour. Beat well. Cover and set aside in a cool place for 30 minutes.

3. Whisk egg white until stiff, and fold into batter just before using.

4. Heat oil in wok. Dip fish pieces into batter and coat completely. When oil is hot, carefully lower fish pieces in until cooked through and golden brown – about 10 minutes. Remove with a slotted spoon.

5. Reheat oil and refry each fish piece for 2 minutes. Remove with a slotted spoon and drain on absorbent paper.

6. Carefully remove all but 15ml/1 tbsp of oil from the wok.

7. Heat oil, add chilli, ginger, garlic, chilli powder, tomato purée, tomato chutney, soy sauce, sugar, wine and water, and salt and pepper to taste.

8. Stir well over heat for 3 minutes. Increase heat and toss in fish pieces. Coat with sauce and, when heated through, serve immediately.

TIME: Preparation takes 40 minutes, cooking takes 30 minutes.

COOK'S TIP: Choose your favourite type of fish for this recipe.

STEWED CHICKEN AND PINEAPPLE

Pineapple complements the chicken wonderfully in this dish.

SERVES 2-3

Seasoning
30ml/2 tbsps light soy sauce
15ml/1 tbsp oil
15g/1 tbsp cornflour
5g/1 tsp salt
½ tsp sesame oil
30ml/2 tbsps water

750g/1½lbs boned chicken breast, cut
  into cubes

Sauce
7.5ml/1½ tsps cornflour
250ml/8 fl oz water or chicken stock
10ml/2 tsps dark soy sauce
Salt to taste

30ml/2 tbsps oil
1 onion, peeled and cut into chunks
2 spring onions, finely chopped
2.5cm/1 inch fresh root ginger, peeled and
  thinly sliced
4-5 pineapple rings, cut into chunks

1. Mix the seasoning ingredients together.

2. Add the cubed chicken and marinate for 10-12 minutes.

3. Mix the sauce ingredients together together in a bowl.

4. Heat the oil in a wok and fry the onions for 2 minutes until just tender. Add the drained chicken and fry for 3-4 minutes.

5. Add the root ginger and fry for 1 minute.

6. Add any remaining marinade and the sauce ingredients and bring to the boil. Cook stirring, until the sauce thickens then add the pineapple chunks. Heat through. Remove from the heat and serve with fried rice.

TIME: Preparation takes 30 minutes, cooking takes 15 minutes.

Soy Chicken Wings

These delicious chicken wings can be served on any occasion.

SERVES 4

1kg/2lbs chicken wings
½ tsp crushed root ginger
15ml/1 tbsp light soy sauce
15ml/1 tbsp sugar
5g/1 tsp cornflour
10ml/2 tsps sesame oil
15ml/1 tbsp Chinese wine, or 30ml/
  2 tbsps dry sherry
Salt
Pepper
30ml/2 tbsps peanut oil
2 spring onions, sliced
15ml/1 tbsp dark soy sauce
1 star anise
45ml/3 tbsps water

1. Wash chicken wings and dry on absorbent paper.

2. Mix together ginger, light soy sauce, sugar, cornflour, sesame oil, wine, and seasoning. Pour marinade over chicken wings and leave for at least 1 hour, turning occasionally.

3. Heat peanut oil until very hot. Add spring onions and chicken wings, and fry until chicken is browned well on all sides.

4. Add dark soy sauce, star anise and water. Bring to the boil, and simmer for 15 minutes.

5. Remove star anise. Serve hot or cold.

TIME: Preparation takes 1 hour 10 minutes, cooking takes 20 minutes.

BUYING GUIDE: Peanut oil and sesame oil should both be available from supermarkets.

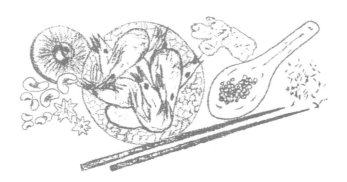

CHICKEN AND CASHEW NUTS

A popular combination that works extremely well.

SERVES 4

350g/12oz chicken breast, sliced into
   2.4cm/1-inch pieces
15g/1 tbsp cornflour

Seasoning
5g/1 tsp salt
5ml/1 tsp sesame oil
15ml/1 tbsp light soy sauce
½ tsp sugar

Oil for deep frying
100g/4oz cashew nuts
2 spring onions, chopped
1 small onion, peeled and cubed
2.5cm/1 inch fresh root ginger, peeled and
   sliced
2 cloves of garlic, sliced
75g/3oz mange tout
50g/2oz bamboo shoots, thinly sliced

Sauce
10ml/2 tsps cornflour
15ml/1 tbsp Hoisin sauce
200ml (just over ⅓ pint) chicken stock
Pinch monosodium glutamate (optional)

1. Roll the chicken pieces in cornflour. Discard the remaining cornflour.

2. Mix the seasoning ingredients together and pour over chicken. Leave to stand for 10 minutes.

3. Heat oil for deep frying and fry cashew nuts until golden brown. Remove the nuts and drain on kitchen paper.

4. Heat 30ml/2 tbsps oil in a wok and stir-fry the onions, ginger and garlic for 2-3 minutes.

5. Add mange tout and bamboo shoots and stir-fry for 3 minutes. Remove the fried ingredients.

6. Add 15ml/1 tbsp oil to the wok and fry the chicken for 3-4 minutes. Remove the chicken.

7. Clean the wok and add a further 10ml/ 2 tsps oil and return chicken, cashew nuts and fried onions etc. to the wok.

8. Prepare the sauce by mixing the cornflour, Hoisin sauce, chicken stock and monosodium glutamate together.

9. Pour over the chicken. Mix well and cook until the sauce thickens and becomes transparent.

TIME: Preparation takes 15 minutes, cooking takes 15 minutes.

VARIATION: A few chunks of pineapple will add extra zest to the dish.

STEAMED CHICKEN

*A great method of cooking chicken and
one which brings out all its flavour.*

SERVES 3-4

750g/1½lbs boned chicken

Seasoning
15ml/1 tbsp light soy sauce
5g/1 tsp brown sugar
5g/1 tsp salt
15g/1 tbsp cornflour
30ml/2 tbsps oil or cooked oil
½ tsp monosodium glutamate (optional)

100g/4oz dried mushrooms, soaked in
  boiling water for 5 minutes and sliced,
  or ordinary mushrooms
1cm/½ inch fresh root ginger, peeled and
  sliced
4 spring onions, finely chopped
30ml/2 tbsps stock or water, if needed

1. Cut the chicken into 2.5cm/1-inch pieces. Mix the seasoning ingredients together and mix with the chicken. Leave to marinate for 15 minutes.

2. Place a plate in a steamer and put the chicken, mushrooms, ginger, half the onion and the stock on top. Steam over boiling water for 15-20 minutes.

3. Serve with the remaining onions sprinkled over the chicken. The steaming can also be done on a greased lotus leaf or a banana leaf. The flavour is quite stunning.

TIME: Preparation takes 20-30 minutes, cooking takes 15-20 minutes.

COOK'S TIP: If you can obtain dried mushrooms do use them as their flavour is far superior to ordinary mushrooms.

ROAST CRISPY DUCK

This dish can be served as a main course for 4 or as a starter for 6.

SERVES 4-6

2kg/4½lbs duck or goose, prepared for
    cooking
60ml/4 tbsps maltose or golden syrup
250ml/8 fl oz water
12 spring onions, cut into 5cm/2-inch
    lengths
½ tsp red food colouring
30g/2 tbsps tomato purée

Duck Dip
100g/4oz sugar
60ml/4 tbsps sweet bean paste
30ml/2 tbsps sesame oil
100ml/4 fl oz water

1. Wash the duck and pat it dry on a clean cloth. Ease the finger between the skin and flesh of the duck, starting at the neck end and working the length of the bird. Put a stick or large skewer through the neck and the cavity of the duck to wedge it securely. This will make the duck easier to handle. Hold the duck over the sink and pour boiling water all over it. Pat the duck dry.

2. Melt half the maltose and dissolve in the water. Stand the duck on a rack over a deep tray. Slowly pour the maltose liquid over the duck. Pour the maltose liquid over the duck 3 or 4 times. Leave the duck in a cool place for 6-8 hours, or overnight, until the skin is dry.

3. Remove the skewer. Stand the duck on a rack in a roasting tin. Preheat the oven to 200°C/400°F/Gas Mark 6 and cook for 30 minutes. Turn over and cook the underside for a further 30 minutes.

4. Melt the remaining maltose with the tomato purée and add the food colouring. Spread over the duck and cook for a further 30 minutes. (The duck should have a crisp, red skin.)

5. Heat the wok and add the mixed ingredients for the duck dip. Cook for 3-4 minutes until the sugar has dissolved and the dip is smooth. Serve in individual cups.

6. Remove the duck skin in squares. Slice the duck flesh and serve with the skin on top.

TIME: Preparation takes 15-20 minutes, plus 6-8 hours to dry, cooking takes 1 hour 30 minutes.

SLICED DUCK WITH BAMBOO SHOOTS

A delightful recipe which mixes some of China's best-loved ingredients.

SERVES 2

1kg/2¼lbs small duck
5g/1 tsp monosodium glutamate (optional)
12.5ml/2½ tsps cornflour
30ml/2 tbsps water
100g/4oz broccoli, chopped
45ml/3 tbsps oil
2-3 spring onions, chopped
2.5cm/1 inch fresh root ginger, peeled and
    thinly sliced
1 clove garlic, peeled and finely chopped
100g/4oz bamboo shoots, sliced
½ tsp sugar
Salt and freshly ground black pepper to
    taste
60ml/4 tbsps chicken stock
10ml/2 tsps rice wine or sweet sherry
Few drops sesame oil

---

1. Cut the duck flesh into bite-size pieces, removing all the bones.

2. Mix the the monosodium glutamate, 7.5ml/1½tsps cornflour and 1 tbsp water together. Stir into the duck. Marinate for 20 minutes.

3. Cook the broccoli in boiling water for 1 minute. Drain thoroughly.

4. Heat the wok and add the oil. Stir-fry the onions, ginger, garlic and bamboo shoots for 1-2 minutes.

5. Add the duck pieces and stir-fry for 2-3 minutes. Add the sugar, salt and pepper to taste, stock, rice wine, sesame oil and broccoli. Stir-fry for 3 minutes.

6. Add the remaining cornflour and water blended together. Stir over the heat until the sauce thickens. Serve immediately.

COOK'S TIP: Fresh root ginger keeps well if tightly wrapped in plastic wrap and stored in the refrigerator.

DEEP-FRIED CRISPY CHICKEN

Everybody loves fried chicken and this recipe is especially tasty.

SERVES 4

1.5kg/3-4lbs chicken, prepared for
  cooking

Seasoning
5g/1 tsp salt
½ tsp five-spice powder
40g/1½oz maltose
30ml/2 tbsps malt vinegar
140ml/¼ pint white vinegar
Oil for deep frying

1. Wash the chicken and hang it up by a hook to drain and dry. The skin will dry quickly. Pour boiling water over the chicken 4-5 times, to partially cook the skin. This will make the skin crisp during frying. Rub salt and five-spice powder well inside the chicken cavity.

2. Dissolve the maltose and vinegars in a pan over a gentle heat. Pour over the chicken. Repeat several times, catching the maltose solution in a drip tray.

3. Leave the chicken to hang and dry for 1½-2 hours, until the skin is smooth and shiny.

4. Heat the oil for deep frying. Deep-fry the chicken for 10 minutes. Ladle hot oil carefully over the chicken continually, until the chicken is deep brown in colour. (The skin puffs out slightly.)

5. Cook for a further 3-4 minutes and remove from the oil. Drain on absorbent paper. Cut into small pieces and serve with a dip.

TIME: Preparation takes 3 hours, cooking takes 13-14 minutes.

COOKS TIP: Maltose is similar to molasses and can be substituted by honey, treacle or golden syrup.

CHICKEN AND BEAN SPROUT SALAD

Steamed chicken and bean sprouts, coated in a refreshingly light sauce.

SERVES 4

175g/6oz bean sprouts
340g/12oz chicken breast meat
15ml/1 tbsp soy sauce
30g/2 tbsps chopped chives
15ml/1 tbsp white wine vinegar
5g/1 tsp sugar
5ml/1 tbsp soy sauce
Pinch chopped garlic
15ml/1 tbsp peanut oil
½ tsp sesame oil
Salt and pepper

1. Cook the bean sprouts for 2 minutes in boiling water. Drain and refresh under cold water. Set aside to drain completely.

2. Sprinkle the chicken with 1 tsp soy sauce and cook in a Chinese steamer.

3. Once the chicken is cooked, set it aside to cool and then slice thinly.

4. Prepare the sauce by mixing together the remaining ingredients and seasoning with a little salt and pepper. Allow the sauce to stand for 20 minutes.

5. Mix together the bean sprouts and the chicken. Pour over the sauce and serve.

TIME: Preparation takes about 15 minutes and cooking also takes about 15 minutes.

VARIATION: The chicken could be cooked in stock, to which the soy sauce has been added.

COOK'S TIP: Mix together the sauce ingredients the day before using them. The flavours will have more time to develop fully.

SZECHUAN CHILLI CHICKEN

If you like chillies this is sure to become a favourite.

SERVES 3-4

340g/¾lb chicken breast meat, cooked
5g/1 tsp salt
1 egg white
75ml/5 tbsps oil
1½ tbsps cornflour
2 slices ginger root
2 small dried chilli peppers
2 green or red peppers
2 fresh chilli peppers
30ml/2 tbsps soy sauce
30ml/2 tbsps wine vinegar

---

1. Cut the chicken into bite-sized pieces. Add the salt, egg white, 1 tbsp oil, and cornflour. Mix and rub these evenly over the chicken pieces to form a thin coating.

2. Chop the ginger, and dried chilli. Cut the peppers into bite-sized pieces.

3. Heat the remaining oil in a wok. Add the ginger and chilli peppers stir-fry for 1 minute.

4. Add the chicken pieces, separating them while stirring. Add the pepper, soy sauce and vinegar; fry for a further 2 minutes.

5. Serve immediately with rice.

TIME: Preparation takes 5 minutes, cooking takes 5 minutes.

COOK'S TIP: Vary the amount of chilli peppers according to how hot you like your food!

PORK WITH GREEN PEPPERS

A quickly-prepared stir-fried pork dish with
green peppers and a Hoisin-based sauce.

SERVES 4

450g/1lb pork fillet
30ml/2 tbsps oil
½ tsp chopped garlic
2 green peppers, seeded and cut into thin
   matchsticks
5ml/1 tsp wine vinegar
30ml/2 tbsps chicken stock
15ml/1 tbsp Hoisin sauce
Salt and pepper
5g/1 tsp cornflour, combined with a little
   water

1. Slice the pork thinly, then cut into narrow strips. Heat the oil in a wok. Add the garlic, green pepper and the meat. Stir together well. Cook for 1 minute, shaking the wok occasionally.

2. Stir in the vinegar, stock and Hoisin sauce. Season to taste with salt and pepper. Cook for 3 minutes.

3. Stir in the cornflour and cook, stirring continuously, until the desired consistency is reached.

TIME: Preparation takes about 10 minutes and cooking takes 5 minutes.

VARIATION: Replace the green pepper with a red one.

WATCHPOINT: It is not necessary to add sugar to this sauce, as the Hoisin sauce is sweet enough.

BEEF WITH GREEN PEPPER AND CHILLI

*The classic mix of beef and green pepper is
given extra punch by the addition of chilli peppers.*

SERVES 4

450g/1lb fillet of beef, cut into 2.5cm/
  1-inch strips
Seasoning
30ml/2 tbsps dark soy sauce
5g/1 tsp sesame oil
Pinch bicarbonate of soda
¼ tsp ground black pepper
½ tsp salt

Oil for cooking
2 green peppers, seeded and thinly sliced
1 onion, peeled and sliced
2 spring onions, chopped
2.5cm/1 inch fresh root ginger, peeled and
  sliced
2 garlic cloves, peeled and chopped
3 green chillies, sliced

Sauce
30ml/2 tbsps chicken stock
½ tsp monosodium glutamate (optional)
5ml/1 tsp dark soy sauce
Salt to taste
Few drops sesame oil

1. Marinate beef with the seasoning
ingredients for 15 minutes.

2. Heat 30ml/2 tbsps oil and stir-fry green
pepper and onions for 2 minutes. Remove
to a plate.

3. Reheat wok, add 2-3 tbsps oil and fry
ginger, garlic and green chillies for 1
minute.

4. Add beef and stir-fry for 4-5 minutes.
Add sauce ingredients, mixed together,
and the fried peppers and onions. Stir fry
for a further 2 minutes, remove ginger
slice and serve.

TIME: Preparation takes 30 minutes, cooking takes 10-12 minutes.

Stir-fry Beef with Mango Slices

This oriental combination of ingredients is refreshingly different.

SERVES 2-3

225g/½lb fillet of beef
15ml/1 tbsp cooking wine
15ml/1 tbsp soy sauce
5g/1 tsp cornflour
¼ tsp sugar
¼ tsp pepper
1 large mango
60g/4 tbsps oil
15g/1 tbsp shredded ginger root
15g/1 tbsp shredded spring onions

1. Cut beef into thin bite-sized slices. Marinate in the wine, soy sauce, cornflour, sugar and pepper for 20 minutes.

2. Skin mango, cut into ¼-inch thick slices.

3. Set wok over a high heat, pour 4 tbsps oil into the wok, wait until it's almost smoking. Reduce heat to moderate, stir-fry the beef and ginger for 1-2 minutes. Remove with a slotted spoon.

4. Toss the mango slices in the hot oil for a few seconds, return the beef and ginger, and spring onions. Stir over the heat for a further few seconds. Serve immediately.

TIME: Preparation takes 30 minutes, cooking takes about 3 minutes.

COOK'S TIP: If you cannot get a fresh mango – tinned mango is available from supermarkets.

MEAT AND PRAWN CHOW MEIN

*This chow mein is a wonderful mix
of vegetables, meat and seafood.*

SERVES 4

450g/1lb dried Chinese noodles or broken
   spaghetti
60ml/4 tbsps oil
2-3 spring onions, chopped
100g/4oz cooked ham, shredded
100g/4oz peeled prawns
100g/4oz shredded carrots
100g/4oz green beans, sliced
Salt to taste
5g/1 tsp sugar
5ml/1 tbsp rice wine or dry sherry
100g/4oz cooked chicken, shredded
100g/4oz bean sprouts
37ml/2½ tbsps soy sauce

1. Cook the noodles in boiling, salted water for 4-5 minutes. Rinse under cold water and drain thoroughly.

2. Toss in 15ml/1 tbsp oil. Heat the remaining oil in a wok.

3. Add the onions, ham, prawns, carrots and green beans and stir-fry for 2-3 minutes.

4. Add the salt, sugar, wine, chicken and bean sprouts. Cook for 2 minutes.

5. Add the cooked noodles and soy sauce. Cook for 1-2 minutes. Serve immediately.

TIME: Preparation takes 20 minutes, cooking takes 12-15 minutes.

SPICED BEEF

A classic recipe which requires the best-quality beef.

SERVES 2-3

Marinade
5g/1 tsp sugar
2-3 star anise, ground
½ tsp ground fennel
15ml/1 tbsp dark soy sauce
¼ tsp monosodium glutamate (optional)

450g/1lb fillet of beef, cut into 2.5cm/
   1-inch strips
2.5cm/1 inch fresh root ginger, peeled and
   crushed
½ tsp salt
30ml/2 tbsps oil
4 spring onions, sliced
½ tsp freshly ground black pepper
15ml/1 tbsp light soy sauce

1. Mix the marinade ingredients together.

2. Add the beef strips, ginger and salt, and marinate for 20 minutes.

3. Heat the oil in wok and stir-fry the onions for 1 minute.

4. Add the beef, ground pepper and soy sauce and stir-fry for 4-5 minutes.

TIME: Preparation takes 30 minutes, cooking takes 5-6 minutes.

COOK'S TIP: Fresh root ginger keeps well if wrapped in food wrap and stored in the refrigerator.

FILLET STEAK CHINESE STYLE

Fillet steak is best for this quick-fry recipe.

SERVES 4

225g/8oz fillet or rump steak, cut into
 2.5cm/1-inch pieces
Pinch of bicarbonate of soda
15ml/1 tbsp light soy sauce
5g/1 tsp sesame oil
5ml/1 tsp Chinese wine, or 10ml/2 tsps
 dry sherry
10g/2 tsps sugar
5g/1 tsp cornflour
Salt
Pepper
30ml/2 tbsps dark soy sauce
60ml/4 tbsps water
45ml/2 tbsps peanut oil
2 cloves garlic, crushed
2 spring onions, sliced diagonally into
 1.5cm/½-inch pieces
½ tsp crushed ginger
1 can straw mushrooms, drained
1 can baby sweetcorn, drained
15ml/1 tbsp oyster sauce

Garnish
Spring onion flowers (cut spring onions
into 5cm/2 inch lengths. Carefully cut into
fine shreds, keeping one end intact, and
then soak in cold water until curling)

1. Put steak in a bowl and sprinkle over bicarbonate of soda.

2. Mix together light soy sauce, sesame oil, wine, half the sugar, half the cornflour, and seasoning. Pour over the steak and leave for at least one hour, turning meat occasionally.

3. Meanwhile, make sauce by mixing 30ml/2 tbsps of dark soy sauce, remaining sugar and cornflour, and water. Mix together and set aside.

4. Heat wok, add peanut oil and, when hot, fry steak for 4 minutes. Remove from wok and set aside.

5. Add garlic, spring onions, ginger, mushrooms, baby sweetcorn, and finally steak.

6. Add oyster sauce and mix well. Add sauce mixture and bring to the boil. Cook for 3 minutes, stirring occasionally.

7. Serve hot with rice, garnished with spring onion flowers.

TIME: Preparation takes 1 hour 15 minutes, cooking takes 20 minutes.

PORK SPARE RIBS

A great restaurant favourite which tastes just as good made at home.

SERVES 4

16-20 spare ribs
5g/1 tsp salt
Oil
5ml/1 tsp ginger paste
5ml/1 tsp garlic paste
5ml/1 tsp onion paste
Pinch monosodium glutamate (optional)
5ml/1 tsp light soy sauce
5g/1 tsp cornflour
1 egg
½ tsp Shao Hsing wine or dry sherry
½ tsp chilli oil

Sauce
45g/3 tbsps sugar
45ml/3 tbsps black vinegar
15ml/1 tbsp tomato ketchup (optional)
5g/1 tsp cornflour
5ml/1 tsp water
15ml/1 tbsp dark soy sauce
½ tsp salt
½ tsp freshly ground black pepper

1. Trim excess fat from spare ribs and rub with salt. Add 60ml/4 tbsps oil to the wok and fry the ginger, garlic and onion for 1-2 minutes. Add the spare ribs and stir-fry for 6 minutes.

2. Remove to a dish and add the monosodium glutamate, light soy sauce, cornflour, egg, wine and chilli oil. Marinate for 10 minutes.

3. Prepare the sauce by mixing all the sauce ingredients together in the wok and bringing them gently to the boil. Simmer for 2-3 minutes and add the spare ribs along with their marinade. Stir fry until the liquid is reduced to half its original quantity.

4. Put all the ingredients onto a baking tray and spread out evenly. Bake at 190°C/375°F/Gas mark 5, for 25 minutes. Baste occasionally with the liquid from the tray and oil. The spare ribs should have browned well and be well coated with seasoning. Serve hot or cold.

TIME: Preparation takes 25 minutes, cooking takes 40-45 minutes.

BUYING GUIDE: Monosodium glutamate is available in most good supermarkets.

SWEET AND SOUR BEEF

*The combination of sweet and sour is an
old favourite for Chinese food lovers.*

SERVES 2

Batter
100g/4oz plain flour
7.5ml/1½ tsps baking powder
60ml/4 tbsps cornflour
15ml/1 tbsp oil
45ml/3 tbsps oil
225g/8oz fillet of beef, cut into 2.5cm/
    1-inch cubes
1 onion, peeled and cut into wedges
2.5cm/1 inch fresh root ginger, peeled and
    thinly sliced
1 clove garlic, peeled and crushed
1 green pepper, seeded and chopped

Sweet and Sour Sauce
60ml/4 tbsps sugar
¼ tsp salt
60ml/4 tbsps red or malt vinegar
5ml/1 tsp fresh root ginger, peeled and
    minced
90ml/6 tbsps water
15ml/1 tbsp cornflour or arrowroot
10ml/2 tsps cooked oil
Few drops food colouring
Oil for deep frying

---

1. For the batter: sieve the flour, baking
powder and cornflour.

2. Beat in the 1 tbsp oil and add sufficient
water to make a thick, smooth batter.

3. Heat the 45ml/3 tbsps oil in a wok and
stir-fry the beef for 2 minutes. Remove
the beef.

4. Fry the onion, ginger, garlic and green
pepper for 2-3 minutes in the same oil.
Remove the wok from the heat.

5. Mix the sauce ingredients together and
add to the wok. Return the wok to the
heat and bring to the boil gently. Lower
the heat and simmer gently for 2-3
minutes until thick and clear.

6. Meanwhile, dip the beef cubes into the
batter and deep fry in the hot oil until
golden brown and crisp.

7. Drain on absorbent paper. Arrange in a
deep dish and pour the hot sauce over the
beef. Serve with a chow mein dish or fried
rice.

TIME: Preparation takes 15 minutes, cooking takes 15 minutes.

VARIATION: Thinly sliced carrots, cucumber and courgette may also be
added along with the onion, ginger and green pepper.

STEAMED LAMB WITH MUSHROOM SAUCE

A great combination that should please most appetites.

SERVES 4-6

1kg/2¼lbs boned leg of lamb, cut
   into strips
2 spring onions, thinly sliced
Salt and freshly ground black pepper
10ml/2 tsps oil
2 cloves of garlic, peeled and sliced
5g/1 tsp cornflour
Pinch monosodium glutamate (optional)
75ml/5 tbsps light soy sauce
45ml/3 tbsps rice wine or dry sherry
1 tsp crushed black pepper
2.5cm/1 inch fresh root ginger, peeled and
   thinly sliced
225g/½lb button mushrooms, thinly
   sliced
Few drops sesame oil

1. Put the lamb into a saucepan and add sufficient water to cover. Boil for 5 minutes. Drain the lamb and retain the water. Arrange the lamb strips in a deep dish and sprinkle the spring onions on top. Season with pepper and salt.

2. Heat the oil in a wok and fry the garlic until brown. Remove the garlic and discard.

3. Mix together the cornflour, monosodium glutamate, soy sauce, wine, crushed pepper, ginger and 60ml/4 tbsps reserved water.

4. Stir the cornflour mixture into the oil in the wok along with the mushrooms and cook for 1-2 minutes. Pour over the lamb.

5. Cover the lamb with overlapping foil and tie around the rim. Put the dish in a steamer and steam over boiling water for 2 hours. Serve with the sesame oil sprinkled over the lamb.

TIME: Preparation takes 20-25 minutes, cooking takes 2 hours 10 minutes.

SWEET AND SOUR PORK

This really needs no introduction because of its popularity.
The dish originated in Canton, but is reproduced
in most of the world's Chinese restaurants.

SERVES 2-4

100g/4oz plain flour
60g/4 tbsps cornflour
7.5ml/1½ tsps baking powder
Pinch salt
15ml/1 tbsp oil
Water
225g/8oz pork fillet, cut into 1.25cm/½-
    inch cubes

1 onion, sliced
1 green pepper, seeded, cored and sliced
1 small can pineapple chunks, juice
    reserved
Oil for frying

Sweet and Sour Sauce
30g/2 tbsps cornflour
100g/4oz light brown sugar
Pinch salt
100ml/4 fl oz cider vinegar or rice vinegar
1 clove garlic, crushed
5g/1 tsp fresh ginger, grated
90ml/6 tbsps tomato ketchup
90ml/6 tbsps reserved pineapple juice

1. To prepare the batter, sift the flour, cornflour, baking powder and salt into a bowl. Make a well in the centre and add the oil and enough water to make a thick, smooth batter. Using a wooden spoon, stir the ingredients in the well, gradually incorporating flour from the outside, and beat until smooth.

2. Heat enough oil in a wok to deep-fry the pork. Dip the pork cubes one at a time into the batter and drop into the hot oil. Fry 4-5 pieces of pork at a time and remove them with a draining spoon to paper towels. Continue until all the pork is fried.

3. Pour off most of the oil from the wok and add the sliced onion, pepper and pineapple. Cook over high heat for 1-2 minutes. Remove and set aside.

4. Mix all the sauce ingredients together and pour into the wok. Bring slowly to the boil, stirring continuously until thickened. Allow to simmer for about 1-2 minutes or until completely clear.

5. Add the vegetables, pineapple and pork cubes to the sauce and stir to coat completely. Reheat for 1-2 minutes and serve immediately.

TIME: Preparation takes about 15 minutes, cooking takes about 15 minutes.

VARIATION: Use beef or chicken instead of the pork. Uncooked, peeled prawns may be used as can whitefish, cut into 2.5cm/1-inch pieces.

PORK WITH BLACK BEAN SAUCE

A tasty recipe which brings together classic Chinese ingredients.

SERVES 2-3

225g/8oz lean pork, cut into 2.5cm/1-inch cubes
15ml/1 tbsp oil
1 red pepper, cored, seeds removed, and sliced

Sauce
3 tbsps black soya beans, rinsed in cold water and crushed with back of a spoon
30ml/2 tbsps Chinese wine, or dry sherry
5g/1 tsp grated ginger
30ml/2 tbsps light soy sauce
3 cloves garlic, crushed
15g/1 tbsp cornflour
140ml/¼ pint water

1. Mix together black beans, wine, ginger, soy sauce and garlic.

2. Blend cornflour with 30ml/2 tbsps of water and add to mixture.

3. Place pork in a bowl, and pour over sauce. Toss together well. Leave for at least 30 minutes.

4. Heat wok, add oil and stir-fry red pepper for 3 minutes. Remove and set aside.

5. Add pork, reserving marinade sauce. Stir-fry pork until browned well all over.

6. Add marinade sauce and remaining water. Bring to the boil. Reduce heat, cover, and gently simmer for about 30 minutes, until pork is tender, stirring occasionally. Add more water if necessary.

7. Just before serving, add red pepper and heat through. Serve with plain white rice.

TIME: Preparation takes 40 minutes, cooking takes 45 minutes.

BUYING GUIDE: Black soya beans are available from health food stores.

Five-Spice Beef with Broccoli

A traditional recipe boosted by the addition of five-spice powder.

SERVES 2

225g/8oz fillet or rump steak
1 clove garlic, crushed
½ tsp finely grated ginger
½ tsp five-spice powder
30ml/2 tbsps peanut oil
100g/4oz broccoli florets
Bunch of chives, snipped into 2.5cm/
   1-inch lengths
½ tsp salt
15ml/1 tbsp dark soy sauce
140ml/¼ pint hot water
2 tsps cornflour, slaked in 15ml/1 tbsp
   cold water

1. Cut steak into thin slices, then into narrow strips. Mix together with garlic, ginger, and five-spice powder.

2. Heat wok, add 15ml/1 tbsp of oil, and stir-fry broccoli for 8 minutes.

3. Remove broccoli and add remaining oil.

4. Add meat, and stir-fry for 3 minutes.

5. Add broccoli, soy sauce, salt and water, and heat to simmering point.

6. Mix cornflour with cold water, and pour into wok, stirring continuously until liquid thickens.

7. Toss in chives, stir, and serve immediately with boiled rice.

TIME: Preparation takes 15 minutes, cooking takes 15 minutes.

COOK'S TIP: Five-spice is a compound of different spices which accentuate Chinese recipes.

Szechuan Aubergine

An unusual side-dish which adds extra spice to meals.

SERVES 2

Oil

1 large European aubergine cut into 5cm/
    2-inch long and 1cm/½ inch thick strips

3 cloves garlic, peeled and finely sliced

2.5cm/1 inch fresh root ginger, peeled and
    shredded

1 onion, peeled and finely chopped

2 spring onions, chopped

100g/4oz cooked and shredded chicken

1 red or green chilli, cut into strips

Seasoning

100ml/4 fl oz chicken stock

5g/1 tsp sugar

5ml/1 tsp red vinegar or wine vinegar

½ tsp salt

½ tsp freshly ground black pepper

Sauce

5g/1 tsp cornflour

15ml/1 tbsp water

5ml/1 tsp sesame oil

1. Heat the wok and add 45ml/3 tbsps oil. Add aubergine and stir fry for 4-5 minutes. The aubergine will absorb a lot of oil; keep stirring or else they will burn. Remove from wok and put to one side.

2. Heat the wok and add 30ml/2 tbsps oil. Add the garlic and ginger and fry for 1 minute.

3. Add the onions and fry for 2 minutes. Add the chicken and chilli. Cook for 1 minute.

4. Return the aubergines to the wok. Add the blended seasoning ingredients and simmer for 6-7 minutes.

5. Stir in the blended sauce ingredients and simmer until the sauce thickens. Serve with extra sesame oil if desired.

TIME: Preparation takes 15 minutes, cooking takes 18-20 minutes.

COOK'S TIP: Vary the spiciness of this dish by increasing the quantity of chillies.

STIR-FRIED STICKY RICE

Glutinous rice cooked with stir-fried mushrooms,
ginger and spring onions.

SERVES 4

250g/9oz glutinous rice
30ml/2 tbsps oil
2 spring onions, chopped
½ onion, chopped
1 slice fresh ginger root
4 dried Chinese black mushrooms, soaked
  for 15 minutes in warm water, drained
  and sliced
Salt and pepper

1. Wash the rice in plenty of cold water and place it in a sieve. Pour 5½ cups boiling water over the rice.

2. Heat the oil in a wok and fry the spring onions, onion and ginger until golden brown.

3. Add the mushrooms and continue cooking, stirring and shaking the wok frequently.

4. Add the rice and stir well. Pour over enough water to cover the rice by ½ inch.

5. Cover and cook over a moderate heat until there is almost no liquid left. Reduce the heat and continue cooking until all the liquid has been absorbed. This takes approximately 20 minutes in total.

6. Add salt and pepper to taste, remove the slice of ginger, and serve immediately.

TIME: Preparation takes 5 minutes and cooking takes approximately 25 minutes.

VARIATION: Replace the water with beef stock to give the rice more flavour.

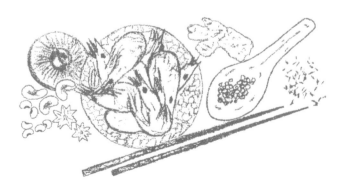

VEGETABLE STIR-FRY

A marvellous blend of Chinese vegetables and nuts,
stir-fried in a little oil and then cooked in an aromatic sauce.

SERVES 4

2 dried lotus roots, soaked overnight in
    water
30ml/2 tbsps oil
75g/3oz bean sprouts
½ red pepper, seeded and finely chopped
½ green pepper, seeded and finely
    chopped
½ spring onion, chopped
1 head Chinese cabbage, finely chopped
75g/3oz dried Chinese black mushrooms,
    soaked for 1 hour in warm water
1 courgette, thinly sliced
100g/4oz frozen peas
30g/2 tbsps cashew nuts, roughly
    chopped
5g/1 tsp sugar
30ml/2 tbsps soy sauce
430ml/¾ pint chicken stock
Salt and pepper

1. Cook the lotus roots in boiling, lightly salted water for 20 minutes. Slice thinly.

2. Heat the oil in a wok and stir-fry, in the following order, the bean sprouts, peppers, onion, Chinese cabbage, lotus root, mushrooms, courgette, peas and cashew nuts.

3. Stir in the sugar, soy sauce and stock.

4. Season with salt and pepper and cook for 30 minutes, stirring frequently.

5. Serve the vegetables slightly drained of the sauce.

TIME: Preparation takes about 10 minutes and cooking takes approximately 35 minutes.

VARIATION: Any type of nut could be used in this recipe, for example walnuts, hazelnuts or almonds.

COOK'S TIP: If time permits, this recipe is even more delicious if the vegetables are stir-fried separately, each cooked vegetable being removed from the wok before continuing with the next. Finish by cooking all the vegetables together for 30 minutes in the chicken stock as above.

PLAIN FRIED RICE

*Producing perfect rice is a must
for lovers of Chinese food.*

SERVES

450g/1lb Patna or long grain rice
¼ tsp monosodium glutamate
30ml/2 tbsps oil
Salt

1. Wash the rice in 4-5 changes of cold water. Drain the rice and put into a large pan or wok. Add sufficient cold water to come 2.5cm/1-inch above the level of the rice. Bring to the boil.

2. Stir once and reduce the heat to simmer. Cover and cook gently for 5-7 minutes until the water has been totally absorbed and the rice is separate and fluffy, with the necessary amount of stickiness to be handled by chopsticks.

3. Spread the rice out on a tray to cool. Sprinkle with the monosodium glutamate. Heat the oil in wok or large frying pan and add the rice. Stir fry for 1-2 minutes.

4. Add salt to taste and stir-fry for a further 1-2 minutes.

TIME: Preparation takes 5 minutes, plus cooling time, cooking takes 10-11 minutes.

STIR-FRIED RICE WITH PEPPERS

*Long grain rice stir-fried with red and
green peppers, onions and soy sauce.*

SERVES 4

175g/6oz long grain rice
15ml/1 tbsp peanut oil
1 onion, chopped
1 green pepper, seeded and cut into small
  pieces
1 red pepper, seeded and cut into small
  pieces
15ml/1 tbsp soy sauce
Salt and pepper
5ml/1 tsp sesame oil

1. Cook the rice in boiling water, drain
and set aside.

2. Heat the oil in a wok and stir-fry the
onion, add the peppers and fry until
lightly browned.

3. Add the rice to the wok, stir in the soy
sauce and continue cooking until the rice
is heated through completely.

4. Season with salt, pepper and the
sesame oil, and serve.

TIME: Preparation takes 5 minutes and cooking takes approximately 25 minutes.

VARIATION: If you like the strong flavour of sesame oil, stir-fry the vegetables and rice in
this instead of the peanut oil.

Watchpoint: Do not overcook the rice in Step 1, or it will become sticky in Step 3.

FRIED VEGETABLES WITH GINGER

*Use your imagination with this recipe and adapt it
to whatever greens you can buy.*

SERVES 4-6

1kg/2¼lbs mixed Chinese green
   vegetables (cabbage, spinach, kale,
   broccoli, Chinese leaf etc.)
50g/2oz mange tout
10g/2 tsps sugar
5g/1 tsp salt
30ml/2 tbsps oil
2.5cm/1 inch fresh root ginger, peeled and
   shredded
1 green pepper, seeded and diced
1 green or red chilli, sliced into strips

Sauce
10ml/2 tsps dark soy sauce
5g/1 tsp sugar
225ml/8 fl oz chicken stock
10g/2 tsps cornflour
5g/1 tsp five spice powder

To Serve
2.5ml/½ tsp sesame oil
Freshly ground black pepper to taste

1. Cut greens into 7.5cm/3-inch pieces.
Bring a large pan of water to the boil and
add the sugar and salt.

2. Add the mange tout and greens and
cook for 4-5 minutes. Drain green
vegetables and discard water.

3. Add 15ml/1 tbsp oil to the vegetables
and keep covered. Heat the remaining oil
in the wok and stir fry the ginger for 1
minute.

4. Add the green pepper and chilli and stir
fry for 10-12 minutes. Add the blended
sauce ingredients and stir well. Simmer
gently for 3-4 minutes.

5. Add the green vegetables and cook for
1 minute. Serve immediately, sprinkled
with sesame oil and pepper.

TIME: Preparation takes 10 minutes, cooking takes 13-15 minutes.

KIWI AND COCONUT DUO

*Incredibly simple to prepare, this recipe is a delicious
blend of kiwi fruit, fresh coconut and coconut milk.*

SERVES 4

4 kiwi fruit
1 fresh coconut
A little sugar (optional)

1. Remove the stalks from the ends of the kiwis.

2. Peel them lengthwise with a small sharp knife.

3. Slice them thinly widthways.

4. Cut the coconut into pieces, reserving all the milk.

5. Cut the coconut flesh into very thin slices.

6. Arrange the kiwi slices on a serving plate and surround with the slices of coconut.

7. Add a little sugar to the coconut milk if desired and pour over the fruit. Serve chilled.

TIME: Preparation takes about 25 minutes.

VARIATION: Coconut milk can now be bought in cans. It is usually of very high quality and is thicker than fresh coconut milk.

COOK'S TIP: The addition of sugar to the milk is optional, and depends upon the acidity of the milk.

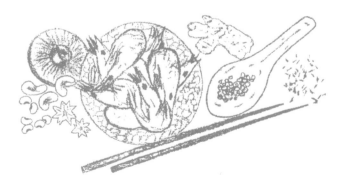

SPUN FRUITS

*Often called toffee fruits, this sweet consists of fruit
fried in batter and coated with a thin, crisp caramel glaze.*

SERVES 4

Batter
100g/4oz plain flour, sifted
Pinch salt
1 egg
140ml/¼ pint water and milk mixed half
  and half
Oil for deep frying

Caramel Syrup
225g/8oz sugar
45ml/3 tbsps water
15ml/1 tbsp oil

1 large apple, peeled, cored and cut into
  5cm/2-inch chunks
1 banana, peeled and cut into 2.5cm/
  1-inch pieces
Ice water

1. To prepare the batter, combine all the batter ingredients, except the oil for deep frying, in a liquidizer or food processor and process to blend. Pour into a bowl and dip in the prepared fruit.

2. In a heavy-based saucepan, combine the sugar with the water and oil and cook over very low heat until the sugar dissolves. Bring to the boil and allow to cook rapidly until a pale caramel colour.

3. While the sugar is dissolving heat the oil in a wok and fry the batter-dipped fruit, a few pieces at a time.

4. While the fruit is still hot and crisp use chopsticks or a pair of tongs to dip the fruit into the hot caramel syrups. Stir each piece around to coat evenly.

5. Dip immediately into ice water to harden the syrup and place each piece on a greased dish. Continue cooking all the fruit in the same way.

6. Once the caramel has hardened and the fruit has cooled, transfer to a clean serving plate.

TIME: Preparation takes about 25 minutes, cooking takes from 10-15 minutes.

VARIATION: Lychees may be used. Organisation is very important for the success of this dish. Have the batter ready, syrup prepared, fruit sliced and ice water on hand before beginning.

WATCHPOINT: Watch the syrup carefully and do not allow it to become too brown.

MELON SALAD

*A refreshing fruit salad, which is especially tasty
served after a heavy meal of many courses.*

SERVES 4

1 large cantaloupe melon
1 mango
4 canned lychees
4 large or 8 small strawberries
Lychee syrup from the can

1. Peel and seed the melon and cut into thin slices.

2. Peel and pit the mango and cut into thin slices.

3. Using a melon baller, cut as many balls as possible out the strawberries.

4. Arrange the melon slices evenly on 4 small plates.

5. Spread a layer of mango over the melon. Place a lychee in the centre of each plate and arrange a few strawberry balls around the edges.

6. Divide the lychee syrup evenly between the plates of fruit and chill them in the refrigerator before serving.

TIME: Preparation takes about 30 minutes.

VARIATION: Use a honeydew melon instead of the cantaloupe variety.

COOK'S TIP: This dessert is best served well chilled from the refrigerator, so prepare it several hours in advance of serving.

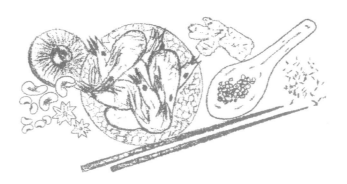

HALF-MOON BANANA PASTRIES

*These crunchy pastries are rather dry, and are
traditionally served with a cup of Chinese tea.*

SERVES 4

Pastry Dough
100g/4oz margarine
450g/1lb plain flour, sifted
Pinch salt
140ml/¼ pint water

Filling
3 bananas
10g/2 tsps sugar
Pinch cinnamon
Few drops of lemon juice
1 egg yolk, beaten

1. Cut the margarine into the flour and
salt. Using your fingers, incorporate the
water gradually to form a ball. Wrap a
damp cloth around the dough and leave it
to rest in a cool place for 30 minutes.

2. Peel and crush the bananas with a fork.
Add the sugar, cinnamon and lemon juice.
Mix together well.

3. Roll out small pieces of dough on a
lightly floured surface and cut into circles.
Place a little of the banana filling on each
round of dough. Fold into half-moon
shapes and seal the edges first by
pinching together with your fingers and
then by decorating with a fork.

4. Continue until all the dough and filling
have been used.

5. Brush the beaten egg yolk over the
half-moon pastries. Pierce the pastries
once to allow steam to escape during
cooking. Cook in a moderate oven, 180°C/
350°F/Gas Mark 4, for approximately 20
minutes, until crisp and golden.

TIME: Preparation takes about 25 minutes, resting time for the dough is 30 minutes and
cooking takes approximately 20 minutes.

VARIATION: Make up the pastries using different fruit fillings.

COOK'S TIP: The cooked dough in this recipe is very crisp. Serve the pastries with a fruit
drink in summer and hot Chinese tea in winter.

WATCHPOINT: Be sure to seal the edges of the pastries thoroughly so that no filling
escapes during cooking.

CANDIED APPLES

Candied fruit recipes are popular in Chinese cuisine.
This one is extra special with a rich batter, and
delicious sesame seeds to garnish.

SERVES 4

3 cooking apples
1150ml/2 pints fresh oil
430ml/¾ pint sesame oil
100g/4oz sugar
15g/1 tbsp toasted sesame seeds

Batter
2 eggs
40g/1½oz flour
40g/1½oz cornflour
Ice water

1. Peel and core the apples and cut into thick circles.

2. Mix the batter ingredients together to make a smooth, thick batter adding water as necessary.

3. Dip the apples in flour and then into the batter.

4. Mix the two oils together and heat to moderate. Deep-fry the apples slices for about 1 minute. Drain and set aside.

5. Heat the oil until it is hot, then fry the apple slices again, for about 40 seconds. This will make them nice and crisp.

6. Pour off most of the oil used to fry the apples, leaving about 3 tablespoons. Add the sugar to this and stir over high heat until the sugar caramelises. Add the apple slices and sesame seeds and stir to coat evenly then remove.

7. Dip the slices into ice cold water to set the syrup before serving.

TIME: Preparation takes about 10 minutes, cooking takes 5 minutes.

Exotic Fruit Salad

Fresh fruit marinated in orange and lychee juice with just a hint of almond.

SERVES 4

1 papaya
1 pomegranate
2 kiwi fruit
4 rambutan fruit
4 canned lychees, plus the juice from the can
3 blood oranges
3 drops bitter almond extract, or ordinary almond extract

1. Peel all the fruit except the oranges, removing pips or pitting each fruit as necessary. Try to buy a fully ripe papaya for the salad. Cut it in half. Using a small spoon, remove all the pips and any stringy skin around them. Peel each half, but not too thickly as the flesh immediately below the skin is very good. Finally, cut the flesh into thin slices or other fancy shapes.

2. Peel two of the oranges. Remove all the pith and cut the flesh into small pieces.

3. Squeeze the juice from the remaining orange, mix this with the canned lychee juice and add the almond extract.

4. Cut all the remaining fruit into slices, rounds or small cubes and combine these with the prepared papaya and oranges in a bowl. Pour over the almond flavoured juices and leave the salad to marinate for a few hours in the refrigerator.

5. Serve chilled.

TIME: Preparation takes about 1 hour and the salad should be left to marinate for at least 3 hours.

SERVING IDEA: Cut a few fresh mint leaves into thin strips to garnish the fruit salad just before serving.

WATCHPOINT: Exotic fruit often arrives in the ships before it is ripe. The solution is to sweeten the sauce slightly before marinating the fruit in order to eliminate acidity.

BUYING GUIDE: If any of the fruits are out of season and unavailable, substitute other appropriate fruit, as desired.

Index